SURFER DAD

CW01466378

SURFER DAD

THE NEW DAD'S GUIDE

TO MAINTAINING A

SURFING LIFESTYLE

Tyler Martin

KP
KAISANTI PRESS
a division of S.S. Publishing Group

Published by Kaisanti Press
A Division of S.S. Publishing Group
Solana Beach CA 92075

SURFER DAD. Copyright © 2014 by Tyler Martin.
All rights reserved.

FIRST EDITION

All information in this book is for informational purposes only. It is not specific medical advice for any individual. All information presented should not be construed as medical consultation or instruction. You should take no action solely on the basis of this publication's contents. Readers are advised to consult a health professional about any issue regarding their health and well being. While the information found in this book is believed to be sensible and accurate based on the author's best judgment, readers who fail to seek counsel from appropriate health professionals assume risk of any potential ill effects. Please note that this advice is generic and not specific to any individual. You should consult with your doctor before undertaking any medical or nutritional course of action.

Cover and interior layout design by Silvia Martinez.

Grateful acknowledgement is made for the rights to reproduce the images in this book: Willyam Bradbury/Shutterstock, S Reynolds/Shutterstock, Greenni, Proskurina Yuliya/Shutterstock, Jamie Meyer, Tom Sandarini

No part of this book may be reproduced in any form or by any means, electronic or mechanical, including photography, recording, or by any information storage and retrieval system or technologies now known or later developed, without permission in writing from the publisher. The only exception is brief quotations in printed reviews. For information, contact Kaisanti Press at info@KaisantiPress.com

26 28 30 29 27 25

TO KOA, SIERRA

AND MY BEAUTIFUL WIFE JEN.

Contents

CONTENTS

Contents

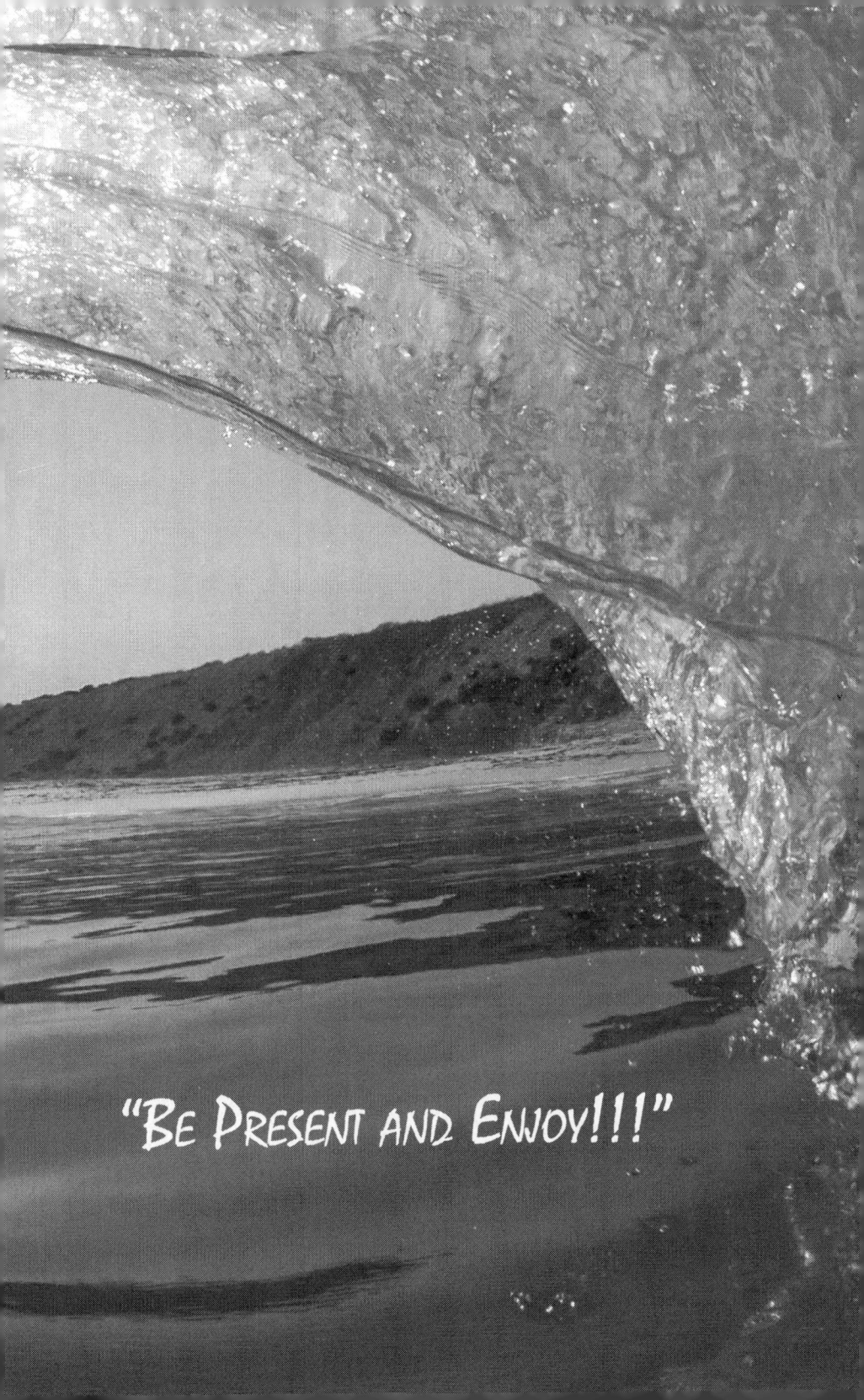

"BE PRESENT AND ENJOY!!!"

INTRO

WELCOME TO FATHERHOOD

Congratulations on becoming a new dad! As a surfing dad, you possess a key to an adventurous, active lifestyle centered around the ocean. This is a special gift that you can pass on to your family that may live on for generations.

Surfing provides an avenue to live a healthy life connected to nature and focused on having fun. Even at the edge of some of the biggest cities on Earth, in the ocean you can find a connection to nature and an endless realm of open space stretching to the horizon. The ocean's playground has free access and is open to anyone. The surfing lifestyle and all that it encompasses is healthy for you and your family.

But to pass on this key to the surfing lifestyle, you yourself need to keep surfing throughout fatherhood. The lessons and tips in this book will help you maintain your surfing during the first few years of being a dad. SURFER DAD will help you discover how small changes and conscious decisions in your life can reveal the best surfer and dad you can be.

Time to Surf

CHAPTER 1

YOUR SURFING LIFE

Attitude is everything,
so stay positive and know that surfing is important
for your soul, your body, and your mind.

Surfing makes you a better dad.

Being a new dad is a busy life. Suddenly your life is filled with so much joy and happiness, and also so much to do. Among the other responsibilities, don't forget to juggle surfing into your routine. Spending time out in the ocean riding waves is one of the best things you can do for your mind, body and spirit.

This chapter offers you tips on how to maximize your surfing time, get more out of your sessions and experience the joy that surfing brings. So read on and let your surfing flourish, even as a busy dad.

CREATE TIME TO SURF

Create time for yourself. Surfing, as unimportant as it seems in the grand scheme of things, is very important. Surfing helps you to be a better dad by centering your spirit, releasing frustrations and giving you time in nature to reflect. Getting out into the ocean, dipping your head under water and riding some waves is the ultimate way to rejuvenate yourself.

Try out these tips to make more time to surf:

The Gift Of Time

There are a couple of guaranteed opportunities every year when your loved ones are asking what gift they can give you- your birthday and father's day. Or, if they are not asking, you can always let them know what you want. The gift is free, everyone can give it to you and it's really valuable right now- the gift of time. How can people give you time?

Ask your wife for a "Surfing Hall Pass" that you can cash in the next time you really want to go surfing. Make sure you ask her to write it out and keep it somewhere safe so there is no confusion when you go to use it. If it's just a verbal promise, it's a lot harder to redeem than a pass you can hand over. Use your good judgment to decide when to use it. For example, if your wife is in the middle of a breakdown, choose a better time to take off and go surfing.

Your friends and extended family can also give you the gift of time. Ask for a "Babysitting Voucher" that you can use the next time you really want to surf. Save it for a great day of waves or for one of those times where you and your wife need a break. The great thing about a babysitting voucher is that you and your wife get a break at the same time. If your child is still really small, you can even ask your friends and family to come to the beach with you and watch your child on the beach while you surf.

Dad Surf Groups

Form an alliance. Put together a dad's surf group where you meet your friends or other surfing dads at the beach and trade off playing with the kids. Since you and your friends probably have busy schedules, agree on a day of the week and try to stick to it.

Choose a friend or group of friends you trust to watch the kids on the beach so you don't have to wonder about how your child is being parented. Also, try to be on the same page when it comes to beach rules so your kids know what to expect during their beach playtime. Bring at least two of each toy and bring snacks for the kids so there are no hunger-induced meltdowns before you get your turn to surf.

Dad surf groups are a win-win for everyone- your kids get to play with each other and socialize, your wives get some time to themselves, and you get to surf. You'll look like a saint with your salt-crusted hair and you will also be surf-satisfied.

CHOOSE YOUR SURF SPOT WISELY

When you only have time for a short session, consider paddling out to a less-crowded spot so that you have the freedom to catch more waves, paddle hard, and get exercise. Sometimes even a quick surf session can be enough to feel completely satisfied, especially if you don't have to spend a majority of the time waiting for your turn. The prime spots attract more people and it's usually because the waves are consistently better there. But that doesn't mean it's always the best place to paddle out. Down the beach, away from the pack, there could be a fun little wave that no one even notices where you can go experience the friction-free glide of surfing all by yourself. Keep your eyes and mind open, and a spot you never expected could give you just the session you need. It doesn't always need to be perfect to have fun!

PREPARE A SURF BAG

Sieze the moment. The great thing about kids is that they always live in the moment. Because kids live in a state of constant flux, you never know when they will lead you to the beach. Having a bag packed with all of your surfing gear ready allows you to stay in the flow as you go out the door without forgetting to bring any of your surfing necessities. That next opportunity to get out there for a surf session might come sooner than you expect. When it does, you can just grab your bag, jump in the car and you are on your way.

There's nothing worse than rushing out of the house, adrenalin pumping, possibly sleep-deprived and getting down to the beach to realize you forgot your wetsuit. Go prepare your surfing bag now!

Here are some items you may need to pack in your surfing gear backpack:

-Your **wetsuit or trunks** (depending on the season and where you live). If your wetsuit needs to hang up to dry, keep your surfing bag next to it so you don't forget to grab your suit on the way out.

-**Wax**

-A **leash** (if it's not already attached to your board)

-**Swim fins** (if the waves are flat, at least you can swim and get the extra workout for your legs)

-**Sunscreen**

-A **water bottle** (not plastic, especially if you are leaving it in a hot car)

-A bag of **trail mix**, a **granola bar** or an **energy bar** (in case you need a burst of energy)

And of course, before you leave your house, don't forget your board!

EXPECT LESS, GET MORE

It's so gratifying to paddle out on an average day and be in the right spot at the right time for a really, really fun wave when you expected nothing. If you just tell yourself that you are happy to get wet, whenever you do get a good wave or score a perfect session, you will be surprisingly stoked. One wave can make your day.

Even if the waves are flat, the ocean has a magical way of making you feel refreshed, so the next time the opportunity arises, jump out into the water with a positive attitude. If you allow yourself to appreciate the simple act of being in the ocean, imagine how much joy you will experience when you actually feel the ocean's energy pick you up and push you into the bliss of surfing.

You never know, a new approach like this might change your attitude, and your surfing life, forever.

MAKE EVERY SESSION COUNT

A surf session is so much more than just the act of going surfing- it's really a combination of activities that benefit your mind and body unlike almost any other sport. By being aware of the different moments of your session and how those different activities can benefit you, you can use every session to strengthen your body, free your mind and stay in surfing shape.

Here are some of the moments you can focus on to get the most out of every session:

Absorb Nature's Beauty

Take moments throughout your session to honor your place in nature and appreciate how blessed you are to be immersed in the ocean.

Enjoy the stillness of the ocean. Let the vast space that extends out to the horizon calm you and free your mind from the daily stresses of life on land.

Look around for dolphins, seals, sharks, and whatever sea life lives in the ocean around you and realize that when you are out surfing, you are part of a different world.

Paddle Hard!

Dig your hands in and really feel each stroke of your paddle. Put your conscious attention into paddling and feel it throughout your arms and back. You can really strengthen (or at a minimum, maintain) your paddling power even during short sessions. After catching a wave, try challenging yourself by seeing how fast and strong you can paddle back out. By paddling hard and using your muscles, you can get the full benefits of the anaerobic aspect of surfing.

Make It Aerobic

There are lots of ways to get aerobic exercise at the gym or on land, but there's nothing better than being in the ocean. Aerobic exercise is good for your heart and endurance because it keeps your heart rate up and delivers oxygen to your muscles.

Surfing is a combination of aerobic and anaerobic exercise, although there are often long stints of inactivity when you are sitting and waiting for waves. Maximize the aerobic benefits of surfing by catching waves in between the sets and paddling more during your session. Stay active, but don't be aggressive.

On the days when you have time for a longer session, don't wear your-self out early. Consider using the longer sessions to build your strength by paddling hard after each wave, instead of focusing so much on making it an aerobic exercise.

Have Fun

Most of all, have fun during your session! The more fun you have, the more rejuvenated and enthusiastic you will be as a dad.

BE PATIENT - THESE ARE PRECIOUS TIMES

Do what you can to stay strong and healthy and keep your surfing as tuned as possible, but also take in these precious times. Appreciate your surfing moments AND your family times. Don't worry about missing the swell of the month if it doesn't fit with what is shaking in your life that month because this time will pass. When you look back on it, being there with your child will have mattered the most.

When you look back on this time period, your child's early years will seem like they were so short. They are such precious years when you get to spend quality time with your child, when you are his or her entire world. One day your child will be in school five days a week and probably want to hang out with his or her friends on the weekends. Since you are your child's world right now, enjoy it and soak up these special times. Be present now and enjoy every moment you can because you only get one chance for your child to be young.

DIVERSIFY

It doesn't matter if you are a shortboarder, longboarder, standup paddler, bodyboarder, or any other type of waverider- trying out another style of riding waves will open up new possibilities for you as a surfer.

The challenge of something new will either inspire you to do it more or bring more gratitude for the way you usually ride waves. The change in perspective can help you understand the ocean better and learn how to enjoy all of her different moods. And riding waves different ways improves your overall surfing.

Practicing different waveriding styles can also help you build strength in areas of your body that are not usually used during your main waveriding style. Remember how tiring it was when you first started paddling a surfboard? With more practice, your muscles developed and your body became conditioned to paddling a certain way. Over time, it takes longer for an activity to have an impact on your body and build strength. By mixing it up and diversifying your waveriding tools, you can experience surfing as a workout all over again.

Most of all, by riding waves different ways, you can learn how to have fun in the ocean no matter what the conditions are, and as a surfer dad, having fun is what you do best.

With all of the innovation in waveriding equipment, there are more options than ever when it comes to choosing a board.

These are some of the best ways to get out into the water and enjoy riding waves in any conditions:

Shortboard

Shortboarding is fast and flexible. Shortboards turn quick and easy. The thinner boards are less buoyant which means paddling a shortboard will help you strengthen your paddling muscles. The speed you can get on a shortboard is a real rush and the ability to do quick turns lets you put your strength into each turn. You can adjust the size, shape and width of your board to accommodate different waves, but in general, shortboards work best in steeper waves that have enough push to get you going. The boards are light and carrying a shortboard to the beach is effortless, especially after carrying your little one and the gear that accompanies a family beach day.

Ride A Fish

The original fish surfboards were short, had wide noses, swallow tails and a twin fin setup. These days, any board that is wider and thicker is often called a fish. Regardless of the exact design specifics, a fish is a great option for a surfer dad like you because it allows you to get speed and have fun on days where your shortboard would struggle to get enough speed. Perfect for summertime or small days, a fish is compact and easy to carry, so you can easily bring it with you to the beach on family beach days. Because a fish is wide and short, it is also a great board to let your child play around on to let him or her experience the feeling of surfing.

Soft Surfboard

Tons of people ride soft surfboards during the summertime and some surfers even ride them year-round. You can pick one up at the big box stores like Costco for $60-$100 US. It's nearly impossible to damage these boards and the boards pretty much can't hurt you either. The extra flotation of the foam makes it easy to learn on, and if you are an experienced surfer, you can have fun on one too. A soft surfboard is a great choice for the entire family if you have to choose one board to bring on a family beach day because everyone can ride it.

Standup Paddle (SUP)

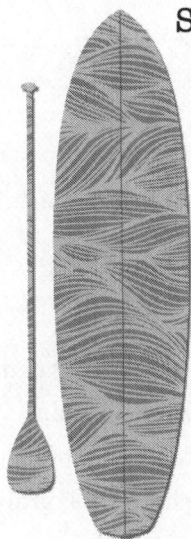

Standup paddling is a great way to cross train because it makes even the smallest, gutless waves challenging. The boards are usually so wide and thick that turning them takes some real skill. After riding a thick SUP on waves, riding any other board feels loose and easy. Even just getting a SUP to the beach can be a good workout because of its weight and bulkiness.

SUP'ing is a full-body workout and you can make it an aerobic exercise by paddling hard and consistently. Or you can take it easy for a relaxing way to cruise along the ocean and see a different perspective while standing on top of the water. Standing up on top of the water lets you see down deeper so you can see lots of marine life while paddling.

After practicing standup paddling for a while, you don't fall very often, which means that as long as the sun is out, you can wear trunks no matter how cold the water is.

SUP'ing is a great way to get your child in the water too. On a flat day, you can bundle your child up in a life vest and take your little one out for a cruise on the water.

There is a lot of room for growth with SUP'ing and if you really get hooked on it, there is no limit to the size of waves you can ride. Because you can get around quickly, you have access to a lot of spots that are out of the way, shifty or hard to reach. This is a big advantage as a surfer dad because you can find uncrowded spots and get out to them. The better you get, the lighter and smaller your board will be so it becomes less of a burden to get to the beach and back.

Bodysurf

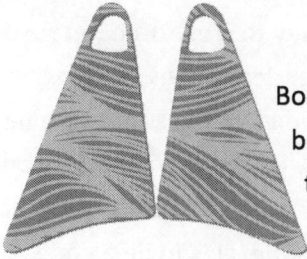

Bodysurfing is the simplest waveriding form because it's just you and the waves. There are two reasons why bodysurfing is perfect for new dads:

1) You can jump out into the ocean at the drop of a hat and all you need are your trunks or a wetsuit and possibly a pair of fins (which you can keep in your vehicle so you are always prepared). If you feel like dipping in the ocean for a quick refresher, you won't need to run home and grab a board to make your session happen.

2) You can catch a lot of little shore break waves in a short amount of time so even a quick bodysurfing session during your lunch break can satisfy your desire to catch some waves. A one-foot wave is head high when you are bodysurfing and the tube only needs to be as big as your head to get a view inside the green room, so the conditions don't need to be epic to have a blast.

You really don't need anything to go bodysurfing, but there are a couple of things that can make it even more fun.

A pair of swim fins can help you get more speed to catch waves and it's better exercise for your legs.

Also a hand plane (a small board for your hand), a fast food tray, or even an old slippa (sandal) can add the ability to do fun little turns while bodysurfing.

Longboard

A longboard opens up the possibility of paddling out on those small days that are too weak for a shortboard. A longboard can be ridden on any waves from nearly flat up to however big you are comfortable riding. Longboards are fun to paddle because they get around quickly and have so much glide. They can get into waves early and are a fun way to throw a little soul into your session.

Because of their extra flotation, longboards are great for teaching your child to surf. Your child can hop on your back or lie on the front of the board and stand up once you catch a wave. Check out the teaching styles for more tips on how to use a longboard to teach your little one to surf.

Bodyboard

The great thing about a bodyboard (aka boogie board) is that you can throw one in the trunk of your car and always have it with you. A bodyboard is pretty tough so you can even throw the stroller on top of it in the car and not damage the board. Bodyboards are really diverse- you can lie down, skim board, stand up or teach your child how to surf on one. If you find some barreling shore break waves, a bodyboard is a great way to get out there for a tube-fest.

A bodyboard is the first way many people ride a wave and is a great way to teach your loved ones wave knowledge before trying out a surfboard.

NIGHT SURF

On those nights when you are craving a surf session and are feeling energetic, remember that surfing isn't only a daytime activity. Night surfing is a great way to get out there for a session if you didn't get enough surfing in during the day. You can help put your child to sleep early and go out for a night session after bedtime. Night sessions are especially handy for those late fall, winter and spring evenings when the sun goes down at the same time that you get off work. The crowds will be light to none, and on a bright full moon, you can see surprisingly well. It will be easier to navigate if you choose a reef that is predictable at a spot you know well. Go with a buddy so you don't spook yourself when you are out there alone at night.

On full moon nights, the moonlight will be your best light source, but you can surf on nights with no moon as well by using a waterproof headlamp made for diving.

"Make every session count to keep your passion alive."

Stay in Shape

CHAPTER 2

YOUR HEALTH

Keep yourself healthy
and your whole family will benefit.

A healthy you makes a happy you
and a happy life.

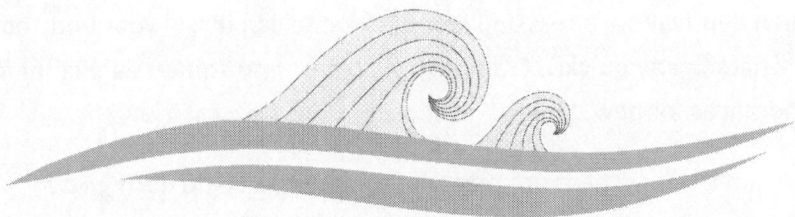

Being a dad gives you even more reason than ever to accept responsibility for your health, to take action and to make daily decisions that will impact your health positively. If you remain conscious of making healthy choices, all of the little decisions will add up to a healthier you.

This chapter focuses on the daily choices you can make as a dad that will make a big difference in your health and ultimately your family's health.

TAKE CARE OF YOUR BODY TOO

When you are a dad, a lot of emphasis is put on caring for your child, and rightfully so. During the first few years, your child requires a lot of your attention and relies on you and your wife for everything. For the first few months after birth, your wife also needs a lot of care because she's just been through more than you will probably ever go through. With all of these new responsibilities, it's easy to neglect yourself. But your health is super important too, so don't forget to maintain and care for your body. Besides being healthy for your family's sake, give your body what it needs to function properly so that when you get out there for a surf session, your body will perform for you.

Sleep deprivation, stress and lack of exercise can throw your body out of whack pretty quickly. Cramping, weakness and stiffness are common hindrances for new dads.

But don't worry, there are plenty of things you can do during your daily routine that will keep your body strong and prepped for your next session. Read on to learn some important things you can do to keep yourself fit through fatherhood.

POSTURE

Try to maintain good posture whenever you can. Maintaining good posture aligns your spine properly, which will reduce your chance of injury. Good posture also allows your respiratory system to work at its full potential, bringing you more oxygen, which in turn helps you think more clearly.

To maintain good posture, you can keep your back straight and shoulders back. Your back muscles are especially important for paddling out, so the better you can take care of them, the better off you will be during your next session.

Follow these easy tips to maintain good posture:

- If you spend time in front of a computer, adjust the height of the screen so that you look straight forward at the screen, not up or down. And always make sure to sit up straight.

- Practice strengthening exercises, like yoga and tai chi. These exercises strengthen your core and keep you flexible, which will lead to better posture.

- When you feel like you need to correct your posture, imagine pushing your chest out from your heart. This will naturally help the rest of your posture align.

- When driving, sit up straight with your back against the seat. A lumbar support pillow can provide extra support for your lower back while driving.

STRETCH

Flexibility keeps you feeling young, improves your balance, prevents injuries and will help you to feel like you didn't miss a beat. Legendary Pipeline surfer Gerry Lopez is a perfect example of how flexibility can keep you going strong. Lopez, in his 60s, has been practicing yoga long before it became mainstream and still outstretches (and outsurfs) most 30-year-olds. His surfing continues to thrive and evolve.

Yoga is one great way to gain flexibility, but you don't need to be in the yoga studio or spend dedicated time on the beach stretching to stay flexible. Once you know what stretches you can do to maximize your surfing, you can do some here and there throughout the day, even while you are picking up a toy, hanging out with your child at home or taking a shower. It's best to perform your stretches throughout the day, not just right before you go out surfing.

Some key areas you should stretch to maintain your surfing are your calves, shoulders, lower back, hips and neck muscles. While stretching, make sure to breathe regularly, move slowly and don't strain yourself.

Here are some simple stretches you can do at home to target those key areas:

Stretch Your Calf Muscles

Step 1. Stand in front of a wall just beyond arm's reach with your feet about shoulder width apart. Place your hands with your palms flat against the wall, also about shoulder width apart.

Step 2. Stretch your calf muscles one leg at a time by first bringing your right leg in front with your knee bent. Move your left leg straight behind you. Keep the heel of your left foot on the ground and push forward into the wall. Shift your pelvis gently forward, toward the wall, and slightly down, until you feel a stretch in the calf muscle of your left leg.

Step 3. Hold the stretch for 20-30 seconds and then repeat with your other leg.

Stretch
Your Hips & Abductors (Inner Thighs)
Side-to-Side Lunge

Step 1. While standing, take a step to the side with your left leg so that your legs are wider than your shoulders and your feet are facing straight forward.

Step 2. Keep hands in a comfortable position to help you maintain balance and support.

Step 3. Keep your head above your shoulders and your back straight. Push off slowly with your right leg, bending your left knee and leaning to the left so that your left leg forms a 90 degree angle (straight line from your knee to your ankle).

Step 4. Hold the stretch for 10 to 20 seconds.

Step 5. Repeat the stretch on the other side.

Stretch
Your Shoulders

Step 1. Put your left arm straight out and bring it over towards your right shoulder, keeping it straight.

Step 2. When you've brought it as far over as you can go, place your right hand or forearm against your elbow and slowly pull your left arm across your body, feeling the stretch in the back of your shoulder.

Step 3. Hold it for 10-20 seconds and repeat this stretch a few times.

Step 4. Then repeat the stretch a few times with your right arm.

Stretch
Your Lower Back

Step 1. Lie flat on your back with your head on the floor.

Step 2. Bring both legs up to your chest and hold them there by wrapping your arms behind the back of your knees.

Step 3. Breathe out while pulling your knees toward your shoulders allowing your hips to come up further off the floor. You should feel a gentle stretch in your lower back.

Step 4. Hold the stretch for 20-30 seconds.

Stretch
Your Hips (Hip-Flexor)

Step 1. Kneel on the floor in a lunge position but with your back knee on the floor.

Step 2. Push your hips forward so you feel a stretch in the muscles in the front of your back leg and hold it for 20-30 seconds.

Step 3. To get even more out of this stretch, raise up the arm that is on the same side as the back leg.

Step 4. Repeat on the other side.

Stretch
Your Neck

Step 1. Bend your head forward and slightly to the left.

Step 2. With your left hand, gently pull your head downward. You should feel a gentle stretch along the back right side of your neck.

Step 3. Hold the stretch for 20-30 seconds.

Step 4. Repeat the stretch on the opposite side.

Stay conscious of keeping your body flexible and you will find that you have lots of stretching opportunities throughout the day.

STRENGTHEN

Use fatherhood as an opportunity to get fit. Turn your daily tasks into a mini-workout. When carrying your little one, the stroller or a car seat, try to do it with strength so you get stronger from these daily tasks. There are lots of opportunities to lift weight and strengthen yourself during your daily routine as a dad. If you recognize these opportunities, you can be a great dad and get a workout at the same time.

Performing a consistent, quick strengthening exercise at home is another good way to keep yourself strong. One quick and easy way to incorporate a strengthening exercise into your life is to do a set of push-ups or sit-ups before bed every night. Doing this takes less than one minute and once you get in the habit, it's easy to keep it going. Another way to sneak in an easy strengthening exercise is to install a pull-up/chin-up bar in one of your doorways. Occassionally, as you pass by, you can stop for a few pull-ups here and there. Everything you do adds up to keep you in good shape.

Within an hour after a hard workout or surf session, feed your muscles with protein to give them the nutrition they need to grow new muscle. Your body can only process a limited amount of protein per hour. Some types of proteins absorb faster and better than others. One of the fastest absorbing sources of protein, which is whey protein, absorbs at a rate of about 8 to 10 grams per hour, so if you are trying to strengthen, eat small doses of protein throughout the day. Nut butters, quinoa, rice and beans, chicken, meat, and avocado are all good, quick sources of protein that you can easily incorporate into your diet.

HYDRATE

Drink LOTS of water, good old pure H2O. Adequate amounts of water keep your joints lubricated and working, your skin healthy, and prevent your muscles from cramping. It's easy to forget to drink enough water, but without it, your body can't function to its full potential.

There is no exact formula to determine exactly how much water your body needs, but you should drink a minimum of at least eight 8-ounce glasses of water a day. Depending on your weight, level of exercise, and lack of sleep, your body might even need more. If you have trouble drinking enough water, buy a water bottle (glass or food grade stainless steel is the best) to keep with you and make sure you drink at least the minimum amount your body needs. Drink pure water because your body can't process other liquids like it processes pure water.

Make sure to drink filtered water and add some trace minerals to replace the minerals that your body needs. You can buy a bottle of trace minerals and add a few drops to your water bottle every time you fill it up. They provide vital nutrients that help your body function to its maximum potential. Lots of people report that adding trace minerals to their water decreases muscle cramping and helps their joints stay healthy.

SUPPLEMENT

You don't want to overload your body with supplements, but there are some that will help keep you strong through the early years of being a dad. Supplements provide you with specific vitamins and minerals that may be missing from your diet.

The following are a few of the most helpful supplements for a new dad like you:

Calcium Magnesium (CalMag)

Muscle cramping can quickly end your surf session and even if you haven't had muscle cramps before, the lack of sleep could bring them on. Calcium and magnesium work together to reduce muscle cramping. CalMag also helps you sleep better by relaxing and calming your nerves.

Vitamin C

Vitamin C strengthens your immune system, keeping you healthier and helping you recover more quickly if you do catch a cold. Vitamin C also helps to eliminate wrinkles, keeping you looking fresh and revitalized.

Vitamin B Complex

B vitamins help to ease stress, give you energy and can be used to treat anxiety and depression. By taking a B-Complex, you will get all eight B vitamins in one pill. Since B vitamins give you energy, make sure to take your B-Complex in the morning so it doesn't keep you awake at night.

Omega 3, 6, 9

Omega fatty acids help in the function of all body systems. As well as many other benefits, omega 3 can improve brain function, which always comes in handy. Look for an omega supplement that has been molecularly distilled, which will ensure that it is free of toxins.

Zinc

Zinc is an essential element that provides, among other benefits, strong immune system support. If you are feeling a cold or flu coming on, a small dose of zinc can help your body keep it away. If you do catch a cold, zinc has also been proven to reduce the duration of a cold, so this is a great mineral to have on hand for you and your family's sake.

Grapefruit Seed Extract

This antifungal, antiviral potent extract from grapefruit seeds can be taken when you start to feel a cold or flu coming on and can sometimes zap it away. When diluted, it can be used topically to prevent infections from cuts. It's good to always have a bottle with you, especially when you are travelling.

Vitamin D3

Vitamin D3 can reduce stress and tension, strengthen your immune system, help fight depression, improve skin health by reducing wrinkles, and improve cardiovascular strength.

If you are not getting enough sun, which is especially common during the first few months of a new baby's life, vitamin D3 drops can make up for the lack of natural vitamin D3. Your body makes vitamin D3 from exposure to the sun's ultraviolet rays, so if you are not getting in the sun as much as you used to, you could be low on vitamin D3.

Trace Minerals

As mentioned before, trace minerals can be added to your water to replenish the vital minerals that are missing from filtered water and many municipal water supplies. An estimated 90% of Americans suffer a mineral deficiency.

Trace minerals are a combination of a very minute amount of essential minerals that your body relies on to function. Although minerals comprise only a fraction of your total body weight, they are crucial for many body functions including normalizing the nervous system and transporting oxygen. They also help your body grow, maintain and repair tissues and bones.

HEALTHY FOOD

Fatherhood is a great opportunity to eat healthy! You are not just eating for yourself anymore; you are teaching, and most importantly, showing your child how to nourish his or her body. No matter how much you encourage your child to eat veggies, if your child doesn't see you eating vegetables, your child probably won't want to eat them either. Show your child how to eat and you will reap the benefits by being healthier yourself and by raising a healthy child.

Don't Know Where To Start?

A good rule that is simple but effective is to eat less processed foods and more whole foods. Whole foods are foods in their natural, unrefined forms. Examples of whole foods include whole grains, fresh vegetables and fruits, beans, nuts, seeds, and fresh wild salmon. These foods naturally contain nutrients that your body needs to not only function, but to thrive. Most of all, follow your intuition and listen to your body to find the right diet for you.

Eat More Fruits And Veggies- Preferably Organic.

Fruits and veggies are a nutritious, delicious and important part of your diet. In the US, Certified Organic foods are grown under stringent standards without using "most conventional pesticides; fertilizers made with synthetic ingredients or sewage sludge; bioengineering; or ionizing radiation", as stated by the USDA. Also, organic standards prohibit the use of GMO seeds. Conventionally farmed foods on the other hand, are often treated with pesticides to reduce crop losses. They are also coated with wax and there is no way of knowing whether they are grown from genetically-modified seeds or not.

If you want to prioritize which organic fruits and veggies to buy because of price, the following list shows you the most and least contaminated choices.

THESE DIRTY DOZEN ARE THE FRUITS AND VEGETABLES THAT ARE MOST OFTEN CONTAMINATED WITH PESTICIDES:

- PEACHES
- APPLES
- SWEET BELL PEPPERS
- CELERY
- NECTARINES
- STRAWBERRIES
- CHERRIES
- PEARS
- GRAPES (IMPORTED)
- SPINACH
- LETTUCE
- POTATOES

BELOW ARE THE FRUITS AND VEGETABLES THAT ARE LEAST OFTEN CONTAMINATED WITH PESTICIDES:

- ONIONS
- AVOCADO
- SWEET CORN (FROZEN)
- PINEAPPLES
- MANGO
- ASPARAGUS
- SWEET PEAS (FROZEN)
- KIWI FRUIT
- BANANAS
- CABBAGE
- BROCCOLI
- PAPAYA

Alternative Milks

Instead of cow's milk, try out alternative milks, like coconut, almond or hemp milk. These milk varieties can provide you with more easily absorbable calcium and nutrition your body needs without the potentially negative effects that dairy has on many people.

Superfoods

Superfoods are foods that are high in nutrients in relation to the amount of calories they contain. If you really want to supercharge your body, superfoods like quinoa, coconut, açaí, and chia seeds are packed with nutrition. Try mixing some of these superfoods into your diet to give you the power to stay strong through your surf session (and to make your family healthier). Superfoods are not only good for you as a dad, but many of them can benefit the health of your whole family.

Try out these superfoods to keep you and your family going strong every day:

QUINOA (pronounced keen-wa)

This supergrain was the staple of the Incan empire, which was the largest empire in pre-Columbian America. The Incans called it "the mother of all grains." Today you can benefit from the high nutritional content of this superfood.

Quinoa is actually a seed, but it is often considered a grain because it cooks and looks like one. Quinoa is the only complete protein grain, is rich in minerals and fiber, and contains all of the 9 essential amino acids.

Quinoa can be cooked and used just like rice, and if you search for recipes online there are tons of ways to add quinoa to your diet. Try making a quinoa salad or using it instead of rice with your favorite meat dish.

Or try the following tasty recipe for a dish your entire family will love:

Quinoa And Black Bean Salad (Serves 4 to 6)
Adapted from "The Whole Life Nutrition Cookbook"
by Alissa Segersten and Tom Malterre

Ingredients
- 2 cups quinoa
- 3 1/2 cups water
- pinch of sea salt (optional)
- 1 cup chopped fresh cilantro
- 1 bunch green onions, sliced (5-8 onions)
- 1 large red bell pepper, finely diced
- 2 cups cooked black beans (if you use canned, rinse well)

Dressing:
- 1/4 cup extra virgin olive oil
- 1/2 cup fresh squeezed lime juice
- 1 tsp ground cumin
- 1 1/2 tsp sea salt or Herbamare

Instructions
1. Rinse quinoa in a fine mesh strainer (check package to see if pre-washed) with warm running water. Place rinsed quinoa in a medium pot with the water and a pinch of sea salt. Bring to a boil, reduce heat to low, cover, and simmer for about 20 minutes, or until all the water is absorbed.

2. Remove cooked quinoa from the pot, place in a large bowl and let cool.

3. Combine olive oil, lime juice, cumin and sea salt in a small bowl. Whisk together and pour over cooled quinoa, toss well with a fork.

4. Add cilantro, green onions, red bell peppers, and black beans and toss again.

COCONUT OIL

Coconut has long been a staple in many countries around the world, but recently, we've really come to understand all of the incredible health benefits of coconut. While coconut possesses many health benefits due to its fiber and nutritional content, the oil is what makes it a truly remarkable superfood.

Coconut oil is anti-fungal, anti-viral, and anti-bacterial. Coconut oil can increase your metabolism, energy and endurance. Coconut oil also increases digestion and helps to absorb fat-soluble vitamins. Coconut contains a high fat content, but the fats are a healthy type of fat (medium chain triglycerides aka MCT's) that actually lowers cholesterol and is burned off as energy.

Coconut oil can also be used as a skin moisturizer and works especially well to treat sunburns. The best way to use coconut oil is to replace your other cooking oils with coconut oil in dishes where the flavor is suitable.

Here are a few creative things you can do to add more coconut oil into your diet:

On Toast Instead of Butter - Simply use coconut oil instead of butter on your toast.

Eat it by the Spoonful - Enjoy coconut oil on a spoon right from the jar. Refrigerate the coconut oil for a firmer texture, add some bee pollen on top (if you are not allergic to it) for extra nutrition and flavor, and scoop it out for a spoonful of superfood goodness.

Smoothies - Add one tablespoon of coconut oil into your favorite smoothie recipe and increase your energy with the beneficial healthy fats that coconut oil provides.

Add it to your Oatmeal - If you like the flavor of coconut oil, add a spoonful to your morning oatmeal.

Or try this scrumptious muffin recipe that uses coconut oil:

Coconut Oil Banana Muffins (serves 12)

Adapted from a recipe by Laura Machell at theGreenForks.com

Ingredients

- 1 3/4 cup spelt flour
- 2 teaspoons baking powder
- 1/2 teaspoon baking soda
- 1 teaspoon cinnamon
- 1/2 teaspoon nutmeg, optional
- 1/4 teaspoon salt
- 1/2 cup MELTED coconut oil (measured while liquid)
- 1/2 cup non-dairy milk (coconut, almond, etc.)
- 3/4 cup coconut sugar (or unrefined granulated sugar)
- 1/4 cup light brown sugar, packed
- 1 tablespoon vanilla extract
- 1 cup mashed ripe bananas (about 2 large)

Instructions

1. Preheat oven to 400°F. Spray non-stick muffin pans with cooking spray or prepare with paper liners.
2. In a large bowl, sift and whisk together flour, baking powder, baking soda, cinnamon, nutmeg, salt; set aside.
3. In a small saucepan, heat coconut oil and non-dairy milk on low, just until the coconut oil has liquefied. Transfer to a medium bowl and add coconut sugar, brown sugar, and vanilla, whisking to combine. Stir in mashed bananas.
4. Pour wet mixture into dry, and fold with a spatula until dry bits are mixed in.
5. Fill muffin cups just over half full, being careful not to overfill or the muffins will spread rather than rise during baking.
6. Bake 16-18 minutes until a toothpick inserted in the center comes out clean.
7. Take pans out of oven and let cool 10 minutes on wire rack before enjoying..

CHIA SEEDS

These little black, white or dark brown seeds are native to Mexico and Guatemala and were considered magical by the Aztecs who used them as part of their diet for centuries. The word "chia" comes from the Aztec word for "strength" and these tiny chia seeds are packed with nutrition. They are high in omega-3 fats, soluble fiber, protein, vitamins and minerals. Anecdotal evidence shows that chia's positive health effects include stabilizing blood sugar, boosting energy and stamina, and aiding in digestion.

Chia seeds are virtually tasteless and are easily digested whole, so they can easily be added to your diet.

Here are some fun ways you can add chia seeds into your diet:

Make chia "gel" - Stir about 1/3 cup of seeds into 2 cups of water. Leave the mixture in the fridge for about 20 minutes minimum to allow the gel to form, but they can continue to soak longer. If you keep the chia gel in a sealed jar, it can stay good in the fridge for up to three weeks. You can add the gel to smoothies, mix it with juice, make pudding out of it or eat it on a spoon.

Drink them - Soak chia seeds in other liquids, like juice or coconut milk, for a fun, nutritious drink with a unique texture that makes drinking them fun.

Eat them dry - Sprinkle the whole seeds on to a variety of dishes for extra texture and the nutritious benefits that chia seeds offer. They add a nice nutritious touch to salads, granola, yogurt, stir fry, muffins, cookies and oatmeal.

Or try the following savory dinner recipe:

Chia Meatloaf (Serves 6)

Recipe adapted from Chia: The Complete Guide to the Ultimate Superfood by Wayne Coates

Ingredients

- 1/2 cup V8 Vegetable Juice, Low Sodium
- 1 cup lentils, cooked and mashed
- 1 cup onions, chopped
- 1 cup celery, finely chopped
- 2 cloves garlic, minced
- 5 tbsp chia seeds
- 1/2 cup of bread crumbs
- 1 1/2 pounds lean turkey, ground
- salt and pepper

Instructions

1. Preheat the oven to 350°F
2. Combine vegetable juice, lentils, onions, celery, garlic, salt and pepper in a bowl.
3. Add chia seeds and stir. Let stand for 15 minutes.
4. Grease a 5 x 9 loaf pan.
5. Add the turkey and bread crumbs to the mixture and combine all ingredients.
6. Put the mixture into the prepared loaf pan and cover with aluminum foil.
7. Bake until golden (about 90 minutes). Remove the foil for the last 10 minutes. Let stand for 15 minutes before slicing.

AÇAÍ (pronounced ah-sigh-ee)

The popularity of this little purple fruit from the Amazon Rainforest has exploded over the last few years due to its dense nutritional content, including antioxidants, essential fatty acids, fiber, amino acids, and protein. The amount of nutrients that this small fruit contains has led it to be considered as one of the top superfoods on earth.

There are many forms of açaí available, but the best way to get the maximum benefit, besides by eating the fresh fruit, is to consume a high quality juice or puree. In addition to açaí's abundant health benefits, the demand for açaí is helping to preserve our ecosystem by providing farmers with a sustainable livelihood without damaging the Amazon Rainforest.

If you haven't tried açaí yet, *this traditional Brazilian style açaí bowl recipe will get you hooked on the little berry's natural energy boost:*

Mango Açaí Bowl (Serves 1-2)

Bowl Ingredients

- 7oz frozen pureed açaí (sometimes also referred to as "açaí pulp" or "crushed açaí"). 7oz is two of the packages that come in a Sambazon four pack.
- 1/2 mango (or a 1/4-1/2 cup frozen mango)
- 1/2 banana
- 1/2 apple
- coconut flakes
- splash of apple or orange juice

Toppings:

- granola
- diced mango
- ½ banana
- hemp seeds
- blueberries
- raw cacao nibs
- dried coconut

Instructions

1. Blend "Bowl Ingredients" on high. Add more apple juice or orange juice if necessary- but keep it thick.
2. Put it in a bowl and garnish with granola and other toppings.

For a bounty of creative açaí bowl recipes, check out Sambazon.com.

If you like the effects of eating these superfoods, also check out some of the other superfoods like farro, hemp seeds, maca, nori and goji berries.

Coffee And Energy

Overdoing it on coffee puts a lot of stress your adrenals, which can end up leaving you feeling extra tired after the coffee buzz wears off. Instead of reaching for another cup of Joe, try an alternative energy booster that is less taxing on your body.

These energy-boosting alternatives might be exactly what you need:

- **WHEATGRASS JUICE.** This little shot of juice is caffeine-free but it will give you a healthy dose of vitamins, minerals and nutrients for a natural energizing effect. You can get a wheat grass shot at a juice bar or most health food stores. Drink it freshly juiced for maximum benefits.

- **GREEN TEA.** Green Tea has less caffeine than coffee and is packed with antioxidants which benefit your body.

- **YERBA MATE.** This South American tea does contain caffeine, but it also contains other nutrients, including antioxidants, amino acids, polyphenols, vitamins and minerals that are believed to give you a clearer caffeine-buzz than coffee.

- **CHAI TEA.** This tea, which is native to India, contains less caffeine than coffee, but its creamy texture is similar to coffee. Just make sure to avoid mixes that are full of sugar.

- **POMEGRANATE JUICE.** This juice is a tangy natural energizer that is full of antioxidants. Mix pure pomegranate juice with mineral water for a refreshing beverage.

- *GREEN SMOOTHIE.* Blend together some of your favorite fruits and vegetables like spinach, kale, blueberries and bananas for a nutrient-rich smoothie that will give you natural caffeine-free energy. Add Hawaiian spirulina for even more nutrition and protein. If you need a starting point, *try out this tasty green smoothie from Cecliia Kinzie at RawGlow.com*

Spinach Green Smoothie

(Simply mix the following ingredients in a blender)

- 1 1/2 cups water or coconut water
- 1 banana
- 2 cups baby spinach
- 3 chopped and pitted medjool dates
- 1/4 avocado
- 1 lime peeled
- 1/2 tsp lime zest
- pinch of xylitol
- 3 cups ice

"Nourish your body and mind so you can be healthy to do the things you love."

Enjoy
the
Beach

CHAPTER 3

THE SURFING FAMILY

Share your love of the sea
with your family.

And your surfing family
will grow.

You ou probably want to jump out into the ocean with your child, push him or her into a wave and start surfing together as a family right away. Yes, it's exciting to share your passion but like all natural processes, things take time. Your child needs to develop a relationship with the ocean just like you have. The ocean is a big mysterious world for your child so be patient as he or she gets comfortable with all of the totally new experiences that the ocean creates- salt water in his or her eyes, going underwater, feeling the currents, the push and pull of the tides, and the sea life that your child can't see below the surface. By being an understanding dad and nourishing your child's developing relationship with the ocean, your family will grow to love the beach as much as you do.

BE MINDFUL OF YOUR MEDIA

Consider the impact of how different media in your life might affect your child's attitude towards the ocean. Take a quick preview before you put on a surf video. Make sure the video isn't filled with scenes of surfers hitting the reef or talking about traumatic surfing experiences. Sensory input like that can have a huge impact on your child even if you don't think your child is paying attention.

One of the major fears for many adults and children is the fear of sharks, and the media prey upon this fear. You can have an impact about what your child sees and learns about sharks by choosing media that informs your child about the life cycle of a shark, a shark's role in the ocean ecosystem, and the many different types of sharks. Preventing your child from having an irrational fear of sharks can help your child grow to become comfortable in the ocean.

THE MAGIC OF BOOKS

Books are a great way to introduce your child to new experiences. There are some great children's books that promote the healthy surfing lifestyle and introduce your child to all of the fun that surfing delivers. Carefully selected books about the ocean also help to bring comfort and familiarity with the watery world above and below the surface of the sea. Collect a selection of books that show how fun surfing can be and try to avoid books that have pictures of scary sharks, sea monsters or gnarly cartoon wipeouts. It's great to provide your child with a variety of fun surfing and ocean-based books, but of course give your child the option to read whatever he or she chooses so that reading remains fun.

The following are a few good books that promote a healthy surfing lifestyle:

The Adventures of Kirra and Rincon. Written by Shelley and Justin Kerr.

Cabo and Coral Go Surfing. Written by Jami Lyn and Udo Wahn.

Cabo and Coral's Secret Surf Spot. Written by Jami Lyn and Udo Wahn.

My Daddy Taught Me To Surf. Written by Joseph Tomarchio.

My Surf Tricks. Written by Roberto Diaz.

Also, check out these ocean-based stories:

Good Night Beach. By Adam Gamble and Cooper Kelly.

Good Night Ocean. By Mark Jasper and Cooper Kelly.

The Surfer and The Mermaid. By Ted Grambeau and Tim Baker.

FUN IN THE SAND

Getting your child comfortable with sand is a great way to encourage a beach-lover at an early age. Some kids love sand right away and some kids take time to realize how fun sand can be. Even if you end up spending lots of time in the sand having fun and playing with your child instead of in the water, eventually a beach-loving child is going to become comfortable enough to start venturing out into the ocean with you.

When you are at the beach, there are some things you can do in the sand that will be fun for you and a blast for your little one.

Check out these fun beach activity ideas:

GET CREATIVE.

Kids love the imaginary worlds you can create with sand. Pile up sand into the shape of a dolphin or turtle and go on a scavenger hunt with your child to find some shells or rocks for the eyes. When it's done, let your child climb on its back for an imaginary ride through the sea. Or you can push sand into the shape of a panga fishing boat for your kid to pretend to set sail into the open ocean.

MAKE YOUR CHILD HIS OR HER OWN BEACH POOL.

Sometimes the ocean is just too rough for little ones so you can make your child his or her own little sea to play in. Dig a hole in the sand right at the edge of the high tide mark so it fills up with water on the biggest surges. Over time, the sun will warm up the water a bit and this will give your child a perfect place to play in the water comfortably without getting rolled around by the waves. It's a nice intro to get your child into the water in a safe way.

CONNECT WITH YOUR CHILD

With all of the technology at your fingertips, it's easy to get distracted during your precious beach time with your child. One of the great things about playing in the ocean is that it's one of the few places these days where you don't usually carry your technology with you. Use it to your advantage: take time to disconnect from your technology and connect with your child. When you can, turn off your phone while you are at the beach. Your child will appreciate the focused attention and crave the precious beach time you get to spend together.

CAPTURE THE MEMORIES

Time passes by so fast and your child will grow while you are blinking your eyes. Make sure to get videos and photos of your child growing up. There are tons of high quality, easy-to-use, affordable cameras for a surfing dad like you to record your family life. As a surfer, look for a waterproof camera so you can record all of those timeless ocean moments from a surfer's perspective and not have to worry about ruining your camera. A hands-free setup, like a chest mount or head strap, works great so you can film without having to sacrifice helping out your child. With a hands-free filming setup, you can be interactive and capture the memories forever.

When looking for a camera that complements your beach lifestyle, consider the following features:

- *Video resolution*- Does the camera record video at 1080p resolution so you can get high quality HD playback of all of your memories?

- *Video frame rate-* Does the camera record video at 60 frames per second for slow motion clips? 24 or 30 frames per second will get you good regular speed video, but you will need at least 60 frames per second for quality slow motion clips. Slow motion is really useful for filming your child surfing or playing in the ocean.

- *Burst photos-* Will the camera shoot a burst of photos with one push of the shutter button? This is especially useful for taking pictures of your child surfing when you are in the water. You can also use this mode to make an action sequence, where you merge multiple photos into one picture for an effect your kids will love.

- *Waterproof-* Is the camera waterproof or does it come with a waterproof case? As a surfer dad, a waterproof camera will let you record your lifestyle and get footage of you with your child in the water.

Check out these waterproof cameras/cases, which are some of the best options for a surfing dad to capture video and photos:

- *GoPro Cameras.* Super waterproof, great video quality, and there is a wide-variety of mounts available. GoPro is the original point of view (pov) camera. The higher end of the range has more features and better settings, but all of the models record high quality video and photos.

- *Waterproof Point And Shoot Cameras.* Nikon, Canon, Panasonic, Olympus and Sony all make great rugged, waterproof cameras that will be able to handle your beach-oriented lifestyle.

- *Waterproof Your Smartphone.* Mophie, Optrix, and Hitcase are a few waterproof options for your smartphone, although there are lots more to choose from. Many of the photography-specific phone cases come with a wide-angle conversion lens so you can get a better perspective of the action. Using your smartphone in a waterproof case is convenient because you usually have your phone with you, but if it gets wet, you're losing a lot more than just a camera. Another downside of using your phone to record your memories is that it might be hard to step away from your responsibilities when you have your phone with you in the water.

- *Other POV Cameras.* Ion and Drift HD are a couple of brands who offer similar cameras to GoPro. If you don't like something about GoPro cameras, check out these brands.

Even if you don't have a chance to edit your videos or photos right now, at least you will have the memories stored. There are lots of priceless moments you will want to keep forever, like the first time your baby touches the ocean, swimming underwater, your first tandem wave and your child's first wave alone.

Make sure to back up your files so you don't lose them if anything happens to your computer because you can't relive those moments.

THE BEACH DAY SETUP

Some of your best family memories will come from those magical beach days where you get to spend hours together at the beach, watching the changing tides and winds. Creating the environment for your family to truly enjoy the beach just takes a few key things so that everyone is comfortable. Once your child gets a little bit older, you won't require as many things to make the beach comfortable, but during the first few years, there are some handy items you can bring to make your beach sessions last longer.

The key is to finding the right balance of supplies and mobility so that you have enough supplies at the beach to last hours, but not so many things that they prevent you from getting there.

The following things will make your beach days longer and make the beach enjoyable for everyone. The more your family loves playing at the beach, the more time they will want to spend there:

Beach Day Supply Checklist

- ☐ Beach Umbrella, Beach Tent or Shade Canopy
- ☐ Queen-Sized Flat Sheet
- ☐ Lightweight Beach Towels
- ☐ Sun Protection
- ☐ A Lifeguard Hat For You
- ☐ Bottled Water
- ☐ Beach Supply Backpack
    - Includes:
    - A few diapers (if your child still uses them)
    - A few baby wipes in a Ziploc bag
    - A small fabric changing pad
    - An extra outfit for your child
    - A small plastic bag to hold dirty diapers
    - Sunblock
    - Your child's sun hat
    - A spare, small lightweight baby toy
- ☐ Snacks
- ☐ Your Child's PFD (Life Jacket)
- ☐ Bathing suits Or Wetsuits for your family

Read on for more tips about what to look for in each item:

Beach Umbrella, Beach Tent Or Shade Canopy

- Find an **SPF or UPF fabric** that will **block the sun's rays** and protect your child from getting a sunburn. Even with proper sun protection, the beach is a bright place so make sure the ambient lighting isn't too strong on your child's face. Before six months, children aren't supposed to wear sunblock, so creating shade is essential. Bronzed bodies look great, but not on a baby.

- The **best** umbrellas or beach tents/cabanas are the ones that can create a **mini half tent**.

- Besides cutting down on ambient light, when your umbrella or cabana is set up as a mini half-tent, it can do a **good job of blocking wind**. It's amazing how the lightest breeze that adults would hardly notice will fling sand all over a sleeping child.

- For a **full beach day**, it is worth the extra effort to bring a **full shade canopy tent**. A shade canopy provides a larger shaded area and you can stand up underneath it. It's almost like having a little house at the beach.

- If you bring a **full shade canopy**, go to a beach where there is **parking close to the sand** so you don't have to carry it too far.

Queen-Sized Flat Sheet

- Lay out a **flat bed sheet on the sand** and then spread your **towels out on top of it** for a spacious play area. Put rocks or something heavy at the corners to keep the sheet spread out.

- The sheet is lightweight and easy to throw in the wash once it gets dirty.

Lightweight Beach Towels

- Find some really *lightweight*, comfortable *beach towels*.

- Using lightweight towels will really *lighten the load*, they *dry out faster* and they create *smaller loads of laundry*.

- As simple as it sounds, this is very helpful, so try to *avoid* using those *big, thick, cozy beach towels*.

Sun Protection

- The safest way to protect your child from the sun is to *keep him or her covered with SPF materials, such as an SPF sun hat and rash guard.* These materials offer continuous protection from the sun without any adverse effects.

- For the areas of your child that are not covered, you may need to use sunscreen.

- The *safest sunscreens* are made with *Micronized Zinc*.

- *Roll on sunscreen "sticks"* are easy to apply *on children's faces*.

- Also make sure to *use sunscreen that will not run* when it gets wet and sting your child's eyes.

- *Apply sunblock before you get down to the sand* so you don't have to tame your excited child and try to keep sand out of the sunblock while applying.

A Lifeguard Hat

- A *wide-brimmed straw hat* not only *protects you*, but also *your child* when you are holding him or her while standing in the sun.

Bottled Water

- *Bring water* so no one in your family gets thirsty and needs leave the beach for something to drink.

- Try to *avoid* using *plastic water bottles* if they are going to be sitting in the sun because the heat can cause the chemicals from plastic (BPA's) to leach into your water.

- *Stainless steel* is the *best option* since glass bottles are not allowed at most beaches.

Beach Supply Backpack (Aka Diaper Bag)

Gather everything you need for your little one into a special beach diaper bag that you always have ready to go. A backpack is a good choice because you can carry it on your back and still have both hands free to carry other beach supplies and your child.

Here are some handy things to put in your backpack:

- A few *diapers* (if your child still uses them)
- A small amount of *baby wipes* in a Ziploc bag
- A small fabric *changing pad*
- An *extra outfit* for your child
- A small *plastic bag to hold dirty diapers*
- *Sunblock*
- Your *child's sun hat*
- A spare, *small lightweight baby toy*

Refill anything you used when you get home from the beach so you are ready for your next beach day.

Snacks

A fed family is a happy family, so keep snacks on hand to keep everyone happy, healthy, and energized. Pack an insulated bag or cooler the night before a beach day and stick it in your refrigerator so you can grab it and go. Or check out the easy snack list below for some ideas of snacks that don't even need to be refrigerated.

Try these no-refrigeration required snacks:

- *Apple and Peanut/Almond Butter:* You can buy single-serving packages of peanut butter or almond butter that don't need to be refrigerated. Spread some on an apple for an easy healthy snack.

- *Trail Mix:* Skip the high-sugar version of trail mix and mix together your own batch. Get some of your favorite nuts and seeds (almonds, peanuts, walnuts, macadamia nuts, or pumpkin seeds are a few options) and mix them together with some sugar-free dried-fruit (raisins, cranberries, figs, blueberries and apples are tasty).

- *Fruit:* Bananas, pears, peaches, mangoes or any of your favorite fruits are easy to grab and go.

- *Veggies.* Baby carrots, cucumber, sugar snap peas, bell pepper or any of your favorite veggies will stay good for the day.

- *Canned Beans (don't forget a smooth edge can opener):* Garbanzo beans, kidney beans, and pinto beans can be eaten straight out of the can for a nutritious snack.

- *Chips or bagged popcorn:* Everyone loves a bag of chips or popcorn at the beach.

- *Make your own Larabar:* Put some dates, coconut and almonds into a food processor and grind them up to a pulp. Shape it into bars and wrap them in parchment paper for an energy-boosting snack your child will love.

Personal Flotation Device (PFD), A.K.A. Life Jacket

A PFD will give your child enough flotation to start to feel comfortable out in the water, and it will keep your child safe. If you already have two children, give the older one a life jacket to wear so he or she can be safe playing at the water's edge. Of course, you or your wife will be watching your little one, but when you go out for a surf session, it will take the stress off your wife.

- For infants and small children, a **PFD should have** a **1) Padded head support** to help keep your child's head above water, a **2) Grab handle** so you can grab your child out of the water or hold on to your child, and a **3) Crotch strap** to help keep the PFD from riding up.

- Look for a **US Coast Guard (USCG) Approved Vest**

- Refer to the manufacturer's size chart to see what size will best fit your child, or try one on at a surf shop.

- Major wetsuit manufacturers like O'Neill and X20 make compact cool looking PFD's so you don't have to put one of those bulky and uncomfortable fluorescent orange life jackets on your child.

POST BEACH DAY TIP- Never fear if your child has been rolling around and tumbling through the sand getting it everywhere. That means your child was having fun, which is what the beach is supposed to be about. After the fun is over and it's time to clean up, rub **baby powder** onto your child's legs and arms **to get sand off of your child's**

skin. To get sand *out of your child's hair*, use a generous amount of **conditioner** in the shower. Rinse well and the sand will wash out with the conditioner.

THE FAMILY SURF MOBILE

The perfect family surf mobile is one that makes it comfortable to hang out at the beach all day long. With a vehicle that you can relax and spend the day in, you and your family can be a self-contained unit, ready for the beach whenever you feel like it. A small RV, camper or camper-van can help your family maximize your beach time and be the ultimate beach cruising family.

Here are some things to look for in the perfect day-tripping surf mobile:

- *A BED.* Having a comfy bed with you at the beach will save you from having to run home for a feeding or a nap. Nap times can easily keep you stuck at home for several hours during the day. But if your child naps in a bed at the beach, you can go surf while your wife stays with your sleeping child and then you can swap and give her a chance to get in the ocean too.

- *A STOVE.* Having a stove in your vehicle allows you to prepare meals and extend your beach days even longer.

With a bed and a stove in your vehicle, you can make it from breakfast all the way through dinner without even leaving the beach.

These are some of the best vehicles to make a family day at the beach really last all day:

- **VOLKSWAGEN VANAGON OR EUROVAN WESTFALIA** (or a VW CALIFORNIA in England). These vans are perfect for a full day at the beach. Features a pop-top with a bed, a stove, and closets. Plus they aren't too big to drive around town on a daily basis.

- **TRUCK WITH A POP-UP CAMPER.** If you have a pickup truck, you can add a pop-up camper to the back of your truck. This way you get to keep your nice truck with its good suspension and add the luxuries of a camper.

- **MERCEDES-BENZ SPRINTER.** These aren't cheap, but they aren't as expensive as you would think. Lots of surfing families have converted these into campers so they can maximize their beach time and have the luxury of driving a Mercedes-Benz.

- **SPORTSMOBILE.** Convert a Ford, Chevy or Sprinter Van into a pop-top campervan with Sportsmobile. It's not cheap either, but it's another great option for a campervan.

- **OLD RV.** Find an old RV (like a Dodge) that has been hiding away in someone's driveway for 20 years, give it a new paint job and you've got yourself a perfect all-day beach mobile.

- **TRAILER.** A trailer is a bit more of a hassle to get the beach, but the good thing is you can detach it from your vehicle when you aren't using it. You'll need to find a beach with enough parking to accommodate the extra vehicle.

Travel and Explore

CHAPTER 4

THE "SURFING FAMILY" VACATION

Explore and create new memories.

Show your child the world through new eyes.

These are the days to remember.

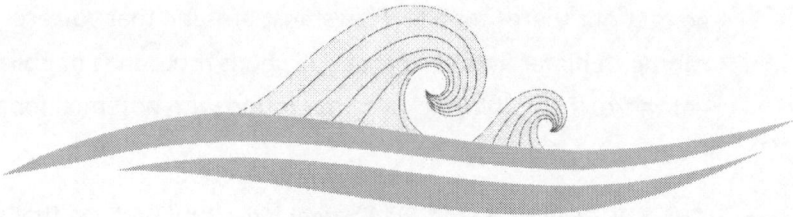

Taking a vacation is a great way to step away from your day-to-day responsibilities to spend quality time with your family and spend time doing what you love to do, which is of course...surfing and hanging out with your family. By making some wise decisions about where and how you spend your vacation, you can easily find the perfect balance that will keep you and your family happy and having fun.

TAKE A STAYCATION

The first trip, and best bet for many families, might just be a *staycation.* A staycation means you take a vacation, but you don't actually get on a plane or drive far away. Going on a big trip with your family may seem overwhelming, but taking time off work to spend quality time with your little one during these precious years in invaluable. You will never get this time back, so take some time off and take a vacation close to home.

There are tons of things you can do that don't require you to go through the hassle and cost of flying or driving hundreds of miles.

Here are a few ideas of how you can make your next vacation a staycation:

- *GO CAMPING.* Find the nearest beachfront campground and go "get out there" for a few days. Just pretend that you are in a campground far away and that you spent thousands of dollars to get there. If possible, pick a campground with potential for good waves.

- *THE RURAL BEACH DAY.* Plan a beach day and pretend that you went somewhere far away. To really feel like you've escaped, you can turn off your phone and try to release your mind from your responsibilities in the office or back at home.

- *HOP TOWNS.* Visit another town near you. Try to find the nearest town that is AS different AS possible so that you can step out of your town's pace. You'll get a whole new experience by leaving your comfort zone. You are probably in the habit of going to the same beaches because you know the routine. Take a chance and go to a beach in your neighboring town.

- *BREAK OUT OF YOUR ROUTINE.* As tempting as it may be to run home to catch up on chores, hop on the computer, or talk on the phone, resist. If you can stay away from your house and out of your typical routine, you will feel relaxed when you return to your normal life.

- *HAVE NEW EXPERIENCES.* Now that you have a new member in your family, focus on being present for the new experience. Even if you think you have done everything there is to do in your area, doing it again with your new family will create new memories.

- *RELAX.* Your child is only young once, so use some of your vacation time to relax and be present with your family. Give yourself a break from juggling work and family life and take some time to just enjoy the family life.

- *KNOW THAT THIS ISN'T FOREVER.* Even if a staycation is the only vacation you can pull off right now, it won't be this way forever. Travelling with a young child can be intimidating. As your child gets older, you will have your motility back and be able to enjoy exotic vacations with your family. Enjoy what it is now and know that staycations are not the only vacations you will ever take.

READY TO GO FURTHER?

If you really want to get a lot of surfing in, take your family on the perfect surf trip. When traveling with your family, you might need to change your idea of the perfect surf trip. It used to be somewhere with your definition of perfect waves and the rest of the details didn't really matter. If you are traveling with your family, you need to be a little wiser about which destination you choose.

Look for somewhere that is family-friendly and has something for everyone. You'll want to choose somewhere where you and your wife can be relaxed. That means different things for different people, so think about what type of travelers you are. Are you ok with being way out there away from everything, or do you want to be down the road from modern civilization? Do you want cold, warm or hot weather? Do you prefer warm or cold water?

Think an exotic vacation to some far off land with perfect waves seems out of reach for you? It's easier than you think.

Consider these compelling reasons to start traveling while your child is young:

- **FREEDOM TO TRAVEL WHENEVER.** Up until the time your kid starts kindergarten, you can travel any time of the year. Once your child is in kindergarten, it's hard for your child to miss much school so you will probably have to travel when everyone else is traveling. Traveling at peak periods means more expensive airplane tickets, more traffic on the roads and more crowded destinations. Take advantage of your open schedule, pick a time when everyone else is in school and go for it.

- **KIDS FLY FREE.** Remember, kids under 2 fly free on most airlines so take advantage of this before you have to buy an extra ticket.

- **KIDS WILL DO BETTER THAN YOU EXPECT, AND GROW FROM THE EXPERIENCE.** Stepping outside of your comfort zone will give you and the rest of your family the opportunity to adapt and grow with new situations.

When choosing your destination for a family surf trip, think about these fine details because they will have a big impact on your overall experience:

- The ideal lodging for a surfing family is beachfront, directly in front of a surf spot. The more convenient it is for you to surf, the more you will be surfing. If you have to drive an hour down a dirt road to reach the surf spot, you won't get out there as often as you would at a spot where you can just jump out for a session during your child's naptime.

- A warm destination makes for easier traveling because you won't need as many clothes and everyone can be comfortable, but you also probably don't want to be somewhere so hot that you are confined to an air-conditioned room.

- Having food available onsite or your own kitchen makes it easy to keep everyone fed. Websites like vrbo.com and AirBNB.com offer a worldwide network of house rentals that allow you to be fully equipped and live like a local.

- If your wife surfs too, try to pick a spot where you both can have fun surfing.

All of the following destinations have lessons available, so if anyone in your family needs some help getting started, you can find surf instructors in the following towns.

FAMILY SURF TRIPS IN THE USA

If you are ready to head out of town, but not ready to leave the United States yet, here are some great family-friendly surf destinations in the USA:

SANTA CRUZ, CALIFORNIA.

Santa Cruz is THE surf town in Northern California. With a wide variety of waves, you can find the right wave for anyone in your family. Although Santa Cruz is also open to south (summertime) swells, fall and winter are the seasons when Santa Cruz is blessed with good conditions and plenty of swell. Steamer Lane and Pleasure Point are two of the most famous surf spots, but there are lots of others once you start searching. The water is really cold, hence the reason Jack O'Neill invented the wetsuit here, but due to its geographic orientation, Santa Cruz is the sunniest spot in the region. Santa Cruz has a long surfing history and lots of other natural attractions for the family to enjoy.

NORTH SAN DIEGO COUNTY, SAN DIEGO, CALIFORNIA.

The beachside towns from Oceanside south to La Jolla are full of sandy beaches and gentle waves for the whole family to enjoy. Each town has its own unique character, but all of them have year-round sunny weather, mild water temperatures and lots of space in the ocean to go surfing. The region has miles of lesser-known sandy beachbreaks as well as some iconic reefs such as Swami's and Windansea. Try to avoid visiting during late spring and early summer when the foggy conditions known as May

Gray and June Gloom keep the coast under a blanket of clouds. Fall and early winter are the best seasons to visit for good waves and typically sunny skies.

OAHU, HAWAII.

Oahu is where surfing began and the surfing history runs deep on Hawaii's most populated island. From November through February, the North Shore gets huge winter swells and some of the world's biggest and most famous waves like Pipeline, Sunset and Waimea come to life. If you are not up for competing with the world's best surfers for waves, there are also lots of other less-crowded spots along this seven-mile stretch of coast.

The North Shore is not the best family destination during the heart of the winter season (November through February) because there tends to be a lot of rain and the consistent big waves make it nearly impossible to get your child in the ocean safely. Late fall (October) or early spring (March/April) are better times to catch moderate-sized waves, less crowds and typically better weather for family beach days.

If you are going to Oahu in the summer, the South Shore is the spot to catch waves when the North Shore goes flat. The gentle rolling waves at Queens are perfect for beginners, so if you are teaching your family to surf, this is a great spot. The stretch along Ala Moana Park has a wide variety of waves that are great for an experienced surfer. If there are no waves, you can standup paddle over the reefs, bodysurf at Sandy Beach or snorkel at Haunama Bay Nature Preserve.

KAUAI, HAWAII.

If you are craving the tropics and want to get away from the hustle and bustle of Oahu, head to the lesser populated Garden Isle of Kauai. There are fun summertime surf spots right in Poipu. With white sand beaches, generally smaller surf and a lot more sunny days than Hanalei on the North Shore of Kauai, Poipu Beach is the perfect family surf vacation. In the winter, experienced surfers will be in heaven up on the North Shore at the variety of spots around Hanalei Bay. The North Shore of Kauai is one of the rainiest places on Earth, so you can expect to see rain if you decide to stay on the North Shore. It's just a matter of how much rain. Shore at the spots around Hanalei Bay.

OUTER BANKS, NORTH CAROLINA.

If you are looking for a domestic getaway on the Eastern seaboard, the Outer Banks has miles of sandy beaches, consistent surf and warm water (in the summer). A narrow continental shelf keeps this stretch of coast open to lots of swell. With some of the best waves on the East Coast and a laid-back vibe, the Outer Banks is a great place for a summertime family surf vacation. Although there can be surf year-round, fall is the best bet for light crowds, warm water and the perfect barrels the Outer Banks are known for.

RINCÓN, PUERTO RICO.

Although Puerto Rico has a vibe of its own, it is actually a territory of the United States. Puerto Rico is a relatively easy flight from the East Coast, but this Caribbean island is a quick way to step into the tropics, even in the middle of winter. The best time to get surf in Puerto Rico is from November through March, which is the perfect time to get your family out of the cold weather and into warm water. The town of Rincón is home to many of the best surfing beaches on the island. While Puerto Rico has a very similar climate to Hawaii, the Spanish-speaking culture makes it a much different experience.

TAKE YOUR FAMILY INTERNATIONAL

International travel can be a bit more intimidating for many new families, mostly because it usually requires a long flight, which many parents dread (check out the tips below for ways to cope with a long flight). Some of you will be ready to head out of the country while your child is little and take advantage of the free flight for children under 2 years old. Others may wait until your child or children are older and a little more independent. Everyone has different travel tastes, so choose a destination that feels right for you and your family.

Once you are ready to step outside of the country borders, these international hot spots are great surf destinations that are perfect for family travel:

ANGLET, FRANCE

Beach life mixes with modern European culture in the beachside town of Anglet, France. You and your family can play on the miles of sandy beaches around Anglet. Anglet has its own share of fun beachbreak peaks right out front and there is a boardwalk for the family to cruise around on if they want a break from the sand. Beachfront lodging, restaurants and snack bars make it an easy family spot with all the flair of a coastal European town.

You can also venture a little further to the legendary beachbreaks at Hossegor, about 30 minutes away. There are also reefs to the south around Guéthary. Biarritz is the next town over just a few minutes away and is also a charming beachfront town with fun waves. You can even take a short trip to Spain's Basque Country and be back for dinner.

September and October are the magic months for good surf and nice weather along this stretch of coast, so if you choose to head to Southwest France, try to make it a fall vacation.

NOSARA, COSTA RICA

Nosara is a laid-back town on the Pacific Ocean side of Costa Rica. While Tamarindo to the north is more well-known, Nosara offers a relaxed atmosphere with a wide variety of consistent sandy beachbreaks and other less-known breaks if you are willing to explore. Jungle-lined beaches and monkeys in the trees promise that you and your family will feel like you are in a true tropical surf getaway.

The best season for surf and weather is from April through July when south swells are hitting and before the rainy season starts in August.

SAYULITA, MEXICO

Sayulita is a small fishing town just north of Puerto Vallarta in Mainland Mexico. With warm water, sandy beaches and that indistinguishable coastal Mexican vibe, Sayulita is the perfect family surf destination. There are great beginner waves right near town and even better spots if you hire a fisherman to take you out by boat. There are also a wide variety of pointbreaks within a short drive from Sayulita.

Lots of ex-pat families live in Sayulita giving it a comfortable beach town vibe. Just avoid staying right near the center of town because the music from the restaurants can be loud, especially for a young family.

NORTHERN NEW SOUTH WALES, AUSTRALIA

Friendly people, typically nice weather, unique wildlife and activities for everyone make Australia a great family destination. The Northern New South Wales coast has warm water and nice weather most of the year. Check out Byron Bay as a good town to set up camp and venture from there. White sand beaches, backed by lush foliage and a variety of waves for every level of surfer makes your decision to pack up and visit this stretch of Australian coastline even easier. Enjoy hiking, surfing, adventuring and checking out Australia's quirky novelties, like the Big Shrimp, the Big Banana and more. Your child can see kangaroos, koalas and emus, although you will probably need to visit a zoo to see the animals up close, especially the elusive koalas.

Although things can be a bit pricey, Australia is English-speaking and very safe so you can easily just relax and enjoy your trip- or holiday, as they say in Oz.

If you want help choosing the right spot for you and your family, Waterways Travel, Wavehunters Surf Travel and SurferLiving.com are a few surf-related travel agencies that can set you up with the perfect spot for you and your family.

TRAVEL TIPS

When traveling to surf locales with your family, there are some things you can do to make your vacation go smooth.

Check out these travel tips to head off any problems before they arise:

WIND

Wind is one potential problem. Because kids are so small and low to the ground, they are especially affected by the wind. Some destinations that you didn't even think were windy will suddenly seem like they are constantly blowing sand in your child's face.

There are a few ways to avoid letting wind ruin your beach session.

- *TIMING.* Go to the beach before the wind comes up. Avoid the windy times of the day and find something else to do when the wind comes up.

- *PROTECTION.* Find a protected spot. Look around for a beach that is protected from the wind, usually by a cliff. Of course, this will be easier in your local area where you know the wind patterns, but finding the right wind-protected spot can make a huge difference in your beach session.

- *SHELTER.* Make a wind block. Tilt an umbrella sideways into the wind to block it. Make sure to secure it in the sand with stakes, rocks, or sand so it doesn't blow away. Once you have your wind block set up and cut the wind out of your beach day, you can sit in the warm sun and enjoy the beach as if the wind isn't even blowing.

LONG FLIGHTS

If you have to take a long plane ride to get to your destination, you need a strategy. Plane rides with a child can bring up lots of anxiety in parents. But, don't let it get to you.

You just need a few things for the flight. Because of all the security, you want to minimize your carry-ons so it doesn't feel like you are traveling

with an extra child. But don't forget to bring the essentials and enter-
tainment for your little one.

- When it comes to keeping your little one entertained during a
  long flight, all is fair game. Depending on the age of your child,
  bring activities that will keep your child entertained, like activity
  books, games or movies. Also, bring headphones if your child
  will need to listen to the audio.

- Bring a distraction for your child. Keep some surprises in your
  bag to pull out when your child becomes bored with a certain
  activity.

- Avoid ear pressure by bringing chewing sugar free gum for older
  kids or a chewy toy for younger kids. For infants, breastfeeding
  during takeoff and landing can help relieve ear pressure.

- Keep your child fed by bringing some snacks for the flight. With
  all of the hustle and bustle, make sure that you keep everyone
  well fed. Of course you won't neglect feeding your child, but
  keep him or her full during travel to maintain a good mood.
  Airplane food alone probably won't do the trick.

"SEE THE WORLD
THROUGH THE EYES
OF YOUR CHILD."

Share
the
Joy

CHAPTER 5

TEACHING YOUR FAMILY TO SURF

Share your love and knowledge of surfing
and give your family one
of the greatest gifts in the world-
the joy of surfing.

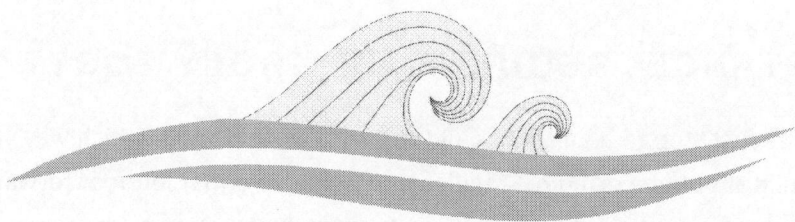

Although you may not be able to start teaching your child to surf right away, believe it or not, that time will be here before you know it. It's good to prepare yourself early and be aware of the various teaching techniques so that when your child is ready to start surfing, you are prepared. You will know the right time when it comes, and when it does, you can finally pass on your valuable surfing knowledge to your precious child.

THE FAMILY THAT SURFS TOGETHER, *SURFS* TOGETHER

Surfing is more than just a sport- surfing encourages a lifestyle. If you want to perpetuate the lifestyle that you love, invite your family to share the joy of surfing with you. Introducing your family to the passionate surfing lifestyle is one of the healthiest gifts you can give them. By getting your family hooked on the ocean, you can all share in the healthy lifestyle that surfing fosters. Picture the future with a surfing family: vacations to surf spots, lots of beach days, and, at some point, all of you out surfing together as a family sharing in the beauty and serenity of the ocean.

STANCE- REGULAR OR GOOFY FOOT?

The first step to teach your child to surf is to determine which way your child should be standing, regular foot (with his or her left foot forward) or goofy foot (with his or her right foot forward). Despite the term "goofy-footed", neither stance is better than the other- it's just a matter of which one feels more natural.

Figuring out your child's natural stance will help him or her learn to surf more quickly because he or she will be balanced and have better control. Usually if a person does large motor skills like throwing or kicking a ball right-handed, he or she will surf regular footed. Left-handers usually surf goofy footed.

If you haven't figured out your child's stance yet, try this technique: Have your child stand behind a line on the ground. Then have your child look at something in the distance and walk towards it. The foot that steps out first is usually the foot that will go in front while surfing. The foot that stays back is your child's 'strong' leg, which is the back foot when surfing.

MENTALLY PREPARING TO TEACH YOUR CHILD

There is a fine balance when it comes to teaching your child to surf. If you are a surfer, you undoubtedly hope your child will want to surf too because you know how much joy it brings. Don't push it too hard though because you could have the opposite effect and make your child NOT want to surf. Here is some advice from other surfing dads about how to encourage, but not force, your child to surf.

- *GET YOUR CHILD COMFORTABLE WITH THE OCEAN.* From a young age, take your child in the water and spend a lot of time hanging out in the ocean. Being in and around the ocean will give your child a sense of comfort. Hold your child in your arms so he or she can be in the ocean but not be exposed to the waves yet.

- *LOOK AT THE OCEAN FROM A CHILD'S PERSPECTIVE.* One-foot

waves look REALLY big when you are only 1.5 feet tall. The next time you are at the shore with your child, kneel down and look at how big the waves look from your child's perspective. It will help you understand if your child is scared of the waves, even though you think they are so small.

- *LET YOUR CHILD SURF WHEN YOUR CHILD IS READY.* Some kids love surfing from the start, others take time to decide if they really are self-motivated to surf. Your child might be into it from the first day or it might take years until your child really catches the surfing bug. Just chill and let your child fall in love with the ocean at his or her own natural pace. You know your child best and will know when your child is ready.

- *DON'T PUSH TOO HARD.* If your child is not into going in the water on a certain day, don't force him or her to. Try to entice him or her into the water by being enthusiastic, but ultimately, listen to your child's wishes. Dragging a resistant child into the water usually doesn't make for a pleasant experience. If he/she isn't into it, take the opportunity to get out there and go surf on your own.

- *TEACH YOUR CHILD ABOUT THE OCEAN.* You are a surfer: share your knowledge with your child and pass on everything that you have learned so that your child can start out with the knowledge that took you years to learn.

- *BE THERE FOR ASSURANCE.* When teaching your child to surf, your main role is to be there for assurance, so let your child know that everything is all right and that you are there for him or her.

OCEAN SAFETY BASICS

As a surfer, there are some basic safety rules that you know like the back of your hand, but these are not so obvious to a child who has to learn everything from scratch. Before you get your child out into the water, remember to teach your child these safety rules. Be conscious of your tone when teaching these rules so that you educate your child, not scare him or her. The goal of teaching your child these rules is to create a positive experience when you are in the water with your child.

- *DON'T TURN YOUR BACK TO THE OCEAN.* If your child can see a wave coming, he or she can be prepared to take a breath and jump over it or go under it. This is one of the basic rules that every child learns and everyone hears. If your child hasn't learned this yet, teach your child this rule and explain why it is important. A fun way to teach your child the repetition of the waves at a very young age is to say hi to each wave as it breaks on the beach. Make a game out of it and your child will learn how waves work while having fun playing with you.

- *WHEN YOU ARE OFF OF YOUR BOARD, (STANDING OR SWIMMING), NEVER PUT YOUR BOARD BETWEEN YOU AND A WAVE.* As you know, if your child puts the board between him or her and the wave, when the wave comes, it will push the board into your child and probably leave a good bruise. Kids learn this lesson quickly once it actually happens, but you can prevent it by teaching your child this rule before he or she gets knocked by the board.

- *WHAT TO DO IN A RIP CURRENT.* A lot of people get scared of the ocean because of rip currents. Teach your child what a rip

current looks like and to avoid swimming in it. It's also important to teach your child how a rip current works. Here is an easy
way to tell your child about a rip current and you can show your
child the diagram below: Rip currents pull water away from
the beach, but they eventually dissipate. If you get in a rip, stay
calm. You can get out of a rip current easily by doing two things.
First, try to swim sideways to get out of the rip current. If you try
to swim against it, you get tired, discouraged and go nowhere,
but if you swim sideways, you will eventually swim right out of
it. Secondly, if swimming sideways doesn't get you out of the
rip, relax and let it take you out to where it ends. Then you can
swim back in, avoiding the spot where the rip is. Teaching your
child these simple tactics can help dissipate any fears about rip
currents.

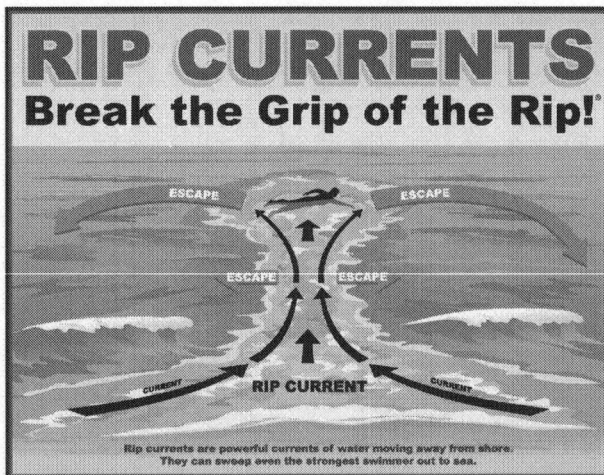

RIP CURRENTS
Break the Grip of the Rip!

ESCAPE   ESCAPE

ESCAPE   ESCAPE

CURRENT   RIP CURRENT   CURRENT

Rip currents are powerful currents of water moving away from shore.
They can sweep even the strongest swimmer out to sea.

IF CAUGHT IN A RIP CURRENT

◆ **Don't fight the current**
◆ **Swim out of the current, then to shore**
◆ **If you can't escape, float or tread water**
◆ **If you need help, call or wave for assistance**

NOW THAT YOUR CHILD IS READY TO SURF

When the time finally arrives and your child is ready to learn to surf, set your child up to succeed. Learning to surf takes patience and persistence, so check out the following tips so that your child's learning experience will encourage him or her to try it again. And again. And again.

- *BE SAFE.* It's easy to get distracted watching the waves when you are at the beach, but when you are teaching your child to surf, always keep a good eye on your child in the water. If your child is not a competent swimmer, use a flotation device, like a PFD, and of course, still keep a close eye on your child at all times.

- *CHOOSE THE RIGHT SPOT.* When teaching your child to surf, be patient and wait for the right spot and conditions. Sandy beaches are perfect for learning so that your child can ride right up on to the beach after a successful ride. You don't want your child to have a traumatic experience, so scope out the set up before you jump into the water.

- *GET THE RIGHT BOARD.* Don't go out and buy a super high performance board for your child expecting him or her to ride it right away. Unless you can be detached and not feel pressure for your child to ride it before outgrowing it, start out with a cheap board that can get dinged up. The last thing you want is to feel like there is a time deadline on getting your child to surf because he or she is going to outgrow that brand new board you just spent a fortune on.

- *KEEP YOUR CHILD WARM.* Everybody always says, "Kids don't get cold". Well, the opposite is actually true. If kids are having fun, sometimes kids just keep going even with mild hypothermia. Some kids mind the cold, others don't. A good wetsuit offers two great benefits- it keeps your child warm even for those long beach days and it protects him or her from the sun. Quiksilver, Roxy, O'Neill and Rip Curl all make decent flatlock seam wetsuits for toddlers. Flatlock seams are perfect for cool water, but they aren't very watertight. Once your child gets a little older, major wetsuit manufacturers make high quality blind stitch wetsuits that will keep your child warm even in winter.

TEACHING TECHNIQUES

Hooray, it's finally time to get out into the water with your child! This is the moment you've been waiting for.

There are several techniques you can use when it comes to teaching your child to surf, and most likely you will be having fun with more than one of these techniques at every stage of your child's development. As you encourage your child to try out these different techniques, let your child choose his or her favorites.

Don't force any of these particular styles, but rather use them as a reference to find what is comfortable for you and your child. The most important thing is that your child has fun learning to surf!

TANDEM ON A LONGBOARD

Surfing together with your child on a longboard is a great way to get your child into the ocean and straight on to the waves. The flotation of a longboard is the perfect surf vehicle to get both of you out into the line-up together. With you lying on the back steering the board while riding the wave, your child can experience the glide of riding down the face of an unbroken wave on his or her first day.

AGE: 1-2.5 years old

> When your child is still light enough to lift up to a standing position with one arm.

TEACHES:

- Gets your child comfortable paddling out and catching waves.
- Balance.
- Teaches your child to be in the lineup with other surfers and to be aware of other surfers.

WAVES:

- Small, rolling and long.

EQUIPMENT:

- Soft Top or fiberglass longboard that is floaty enough so your child isn't getting too wet while paddling and wide enough so you don't tip over.

- If your child is older, you can use a shorter (5-6' long) foam board. When your child stands up on a wave, you can hang on to the back of the board with your legs dragging in the water to stabilize the board.

- A life jacket with a grab handle on the back (most children's life jackets/PFD's come with these).

HOW TO DO IT:

1. Paddle out with your child lying on the board in front of you.

2. Look for a small whitewash or slopey wave that you can go straight on.

3. Keep your child under chest while you paddle for a wave.

4. When you catch the wave, tell your child to jump up while you grab the handle and help lift your child up to a standing position.

5. Ride the wave lying down while you continue to hold on to the handle to help your child balance and ride the wave.

TIPS:

- Only do this in very small waves.

- Look for a spot with a good channel and mellow peak so you can paddle back out without having to go through waves. A (not dangerous) reef break typically has the best channel to get back out easily.

- Your child has to be willing to lie on his or her belly while paddling.

- Hold on tight to your child at all times since you are actually riding waves. You want your child to feel safe and secure with you.

- After you practice this technique and your child becomes comfortable, you can stand up with your child and ride standing up together.

ON THE FRONT OF A SUP

Paddling around together on the front of a standup paddleboard is a safe, very relaxed way to get your child off of the beach and out into the ocean. Since you are right next to your child, you can give your child a sense of security while your child learns to be comfortable on top of the water.

AGE: 1.5-5 years

TEACHES:

- Gets your child comfortable in the water (while barely even getting wet)

- This is a safe way to cruise around and be on the water.

- A great way to see sea life and venture out past the surf zone.

WAVES:

- Flat to 1 foot. Great for the harbor, bay, lake or ocean on a flat day.

EQUIPMENT:

- Large, stable standup paddleboard. 10-12' Long, 28"-30" Wide

- Life jacket/PFD for your child

- Handles on the board for your child to hold on to are optional but may make your child feel more secure on the board. The Surftech Ez Plug Flat Surface Sup Handle or SurfCO Hawaii EZ Plug Handle are two handle options that you can adhere on to your board.

HOW TO DO IT:

1. If you are on completely flat water, put your child on the board right next to shore. If there is shore break, carry your child past the waves and then put your child on the board.

2. Have your child squat on his or her knees on the board in front of the spot where you will be when paddling.

3. Get on the board, being careful not to tip your child off the board.

4. It's easiest to start on your knees so you can be close to your child and hear what your child says. It's also less tipsy. After you both get comfortable, you can stand up and have your child hold on to your legs (or handles if you have them). The goal is not to show off your paddling skills but rather to get your child comfortable out on the water.

5. Eventually you can catch tiny waves with your child on the front of your board. To do this, you will probably need to go on your knees at first or have handles for your child to hold on to.

TIPS:

- Be careful to keep the paddle away from your child so you don't accidentally hit your child with the paddle.

- Make sure your child is old enough so that he or she won't climb off the board while you are paddling.

- Because SUP boards are so thick, it can be hard to go through waves on the board. If you need to walk your child out past the waves while your child is on the board, lift up on the nose slightly to go over little waves.

STANDING WITH YOUR HELP

This technique allows you to stand right next to your child while you teach your child wave knowledge and share your child's first moments standing on a wave. Because you are always holding on to your child and basically eye-to-eye, this is a really fun way to get some huge smiles and have fun with your child before he or she is old enough to be out there alone.

AGE: 2-4 years

TEACHES:

- This technique teaches your child the feeling of riding a wave.

- Also teaches your child to balance on top of the board.

- How to look for incoming waves and general wave knowledge.

WAVES:

- Small and close to the beach with a sand bottom (in about waist deep water is the easiest on you and your back so you don't have to lean over too far to hold your child steady)

EQUIPMENT:

- A bodyboard (boogie board) works best because it doesn't have fins and you can turn it around quickly and easily.
- You can also use a short (5 foot and under) foam surfboard.

HOW TO DO IT:

1. Have your child stand up in his or her natural surfing stance towards the middle or back of the board.

2. Stand next to your child in about knee to waist deep water.

3. Hook your back arm so your child has a "bar" to hold on to. Have your child hold on to your forearm with his or her back hand to give your child a stable support to maintain balance. Have your child hold on to your hand (on your same arm) with his or her other hand. This gives you a good grip on your child in case he or she slips off the board. (See the following diagram)

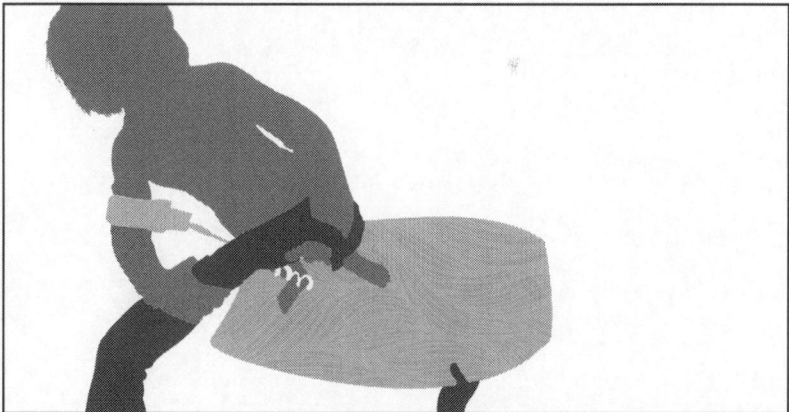

4. With your front arm, hold on to the rail of the board. Use this hand to hold the board steady and turn the board. When a wave comes, use this hand to lift the nose of your board and ride over

the whitewash.

5. At first, you can help your child balance on the board and ride over waves. Once you get comfortable, you can help your child do floaters, pretend tow-ins into waves and airs over the back of the waves.

6. Most of all, be enthusiastic and make it fun.

TIPS:

*   If a "bigger" wave comes or a wave breaks right in front of you, you can lift your child up off the board with one arm and pick up the board with the other hand to get through the wave.

*   Don't hold on too tight to your child's hand so that it is uncomfortable for your child.

LYING DOWN ON A BODYBOARD

Lying down on a bodyboard is one of the easiest ways for your child to catch a wave on his or her own. It's totally safe and at the end of a successful ride, your child can ride right up on to the sand. The important thing is that it gives your child that feeling of riding a wave all alone and this feeling can be enough to inspire your child to continue surfing forever.

AGE: 2-5 years

TEACHES:

- This technique teaches your child the thrill of riding a wave- that weightless friction-free feeling that got you hooked on surfing in the first place.

- This technique also teaches wave knowledge, independence and confidence in the water.

WAVES:

- 1-3' whitewash or slopey waves with a sandy beach, but avoid shore break until your child is more experienced.

EQUIPMENT:

- A bodyboard (boogie board)
- A PFD if your child doesn't swim well yet

HOW TO DO IT:

1. Carry your child and the board (one on each arm) out to the small, rolling waves.

2. For bigger kids, pull your child out on the board and lift the nose to go over the waves.

3. In between waves, put your child on to the board.

4. Have your child hold on to the rails (edges) of the board.

5. Choose a gentle wave and push your child into it so he or she can ride all the way to the beach.

6. After your child finishes riding the wave, show your enthusiasm!

TIPS:

- Don't push your child into shore break waves. If the nose of the board catches in the water and your child slides off the front, your child is going to get a mouthful of water.

- For another fun option at low tide, grab the leash and pull your child on the board across the wet sand. Kids love it. Don't turn too hard through because your child might go flying off on to the sand.

THE STANDING UP TAKEOFF

Your child will really get the full thrill of surfing with this technique. Although your child needs to be confident to be alone in the ocean for a moment after the wave, you child doesn't need his or her own wave knowledge to catch the perfect wave. This is a great technique to get your child hooked on surfing and to start to build your child's independence in the ocean.

AGE: 3-7 years

TEACHES:

- This technique teaches your child the feeling of riding a wave standing up while relying on his or her own balance.

- It teaches your child the thrill of riding a wave without having to use his or her own paddling power or wave knowledge.

WAVES:

- 1.5'-2.5' with a sand bottom for when your child finishes the wave.

EQUIPMENT:

- A short (5'-6') Soft Top foam surfboard.

HOW TO DO IT:

1. Use the standing and holding method from "Standing With Your Help" to get your child out to the unbroken waves.

2. This method is similar to the "Standing With Your Help" technique, except when a wave comes, help your child catch the wave already standing up and then let your child ride the wave alone.

3. As your child is riding the wave, follow your child in so you can help your child get back out after the wave.

TIPS:

- Don't push your child into shore break or hollow waves. Wait for a day with the right gentle waves to get your child started riding waves on his or her own.

- Make sure your child is comfortable and willing for you to let go when he or she catches the wave. Surprises can be fun (like at birthday parties), but not at times like this when you are earning your child's trust in the water.

- Make sure your child can swim sufficiently in case he or she falls off at the end of the wave. Use a life jacket/PFD if necessary and try to stay close.

STANDING IN THE WHITEWASH

This stage marks a huge moment in any child's surfing life. This is when your child is finally able to catch a wave and ride it with his or her own balance and wave knowledge. All of the knowledge and skills that you have been sharing with your child are now firmly planted in your child's mind. Your child's surfing will continue to grow from here. Although the younger years of your child's life will undoubtedly stir up nostalgic memories, soon you will be sitting together in the lineup sharing waves and making new memories.

AGE: 4+

TEACHES:

- This stage is the first truly independent surfing your child will do. Getting up and riding on his or her own is the final phase of the early learning process.

- This technique teaches your child independence in the ocean, which ultimately all surfers need to embrace.

- It also teaches balance and paddling skills.

WAVES:

- 1'-3' rolling whitewash over a sand bottom with enough distance to stand up and ride.

EQUIPMENT:

- A thick Soft Top longboard and a leash.

HOW TO DO IT:

1. For your child's first few sessions on his or her own, swim out with your child to help your child get out far enough to catch a wave. Don't pressure your child to catch a wave until he or she is ready.

2. When a wave comes, if your child still doesn't want to go on his own, you can hold on to the back of the board and bodysurf along with him or her. Try to let your child hear your voice while riding so your child feels secure that you are there.

3. Once your child gains confidence, let your child catch and ride a wave without your help.

TIPS:

- A thick foam board will help your child keep up speed, even in weak waves.

- Have your child use a leash for security, but teach your child that a leash is not a safety device. As you know, you don't want to rely on a leash or your board for flotation.

"SHARE THE PASSION!"

CONCLUSION

LIVING THE DREAM

Every day you wake up, you are presented with a series of little decisions that will shape how your day goes. Now that you are a dad, you will also have a little voice beside you who wants to share your joy for life and experience the world with you. The simple fact that you have been tuned in to the surfing life shows that you are already on a blissful path and that you will continue to adventure on through life.

The way you spend your day is precious. The positive attitude that you carry with you through the day will continue to unveil more positivity. Your ability to adjust and adapt will train your mind to grow with life's ever-changing moments. These are precious times that you have; every moment that you spend with your family and friends is priceless. If you meander this path in health, with an open mind, an eye for the beauty in the little things and with a toe in the ocean, you are living the life you were meant to. Share your love of surfing and your view of life with your little one and ride on surfer dad...ride on.

8849705R10067

Printed in Great Britain
by Amazon.co.uk, Ltd.,
Marston Gate.